FINANCIAL FOUNDATION

Core and Advanced Concepts
for Financial Success

Corey Ganser

CONTENTS

This book is dedicated to my wife and kids, who are my continued inspiration, support, and motivation.

DISCLAIMER

I have over 20 years of experience trading in the stock market, and over 15 years of real estate investing, both leveraging the strategies introduced in this book. I have started businesses (including a personal budgeting business), sold businesses, and been acquired. I have also created and run an emerging technology conference. However, I am not an accountant, tax lawyer, regular lawyer, or certified financial planner. Nothing in this book constitutes financial, tax, or legal advice. I simply provide an overview of key financial planning and investment concepts, along with links to further resources where you can investigate them more.

FOREWORD

Ever since I can remember, I have loved learning about financial planning and investing. I have been doing it for over 20 years and have been very fortunate to implement or explore all the concepts introduced in this book with great success. As a result, I have had many friends and colleagues reach out to me to ask how they should proceed with financial planning or optimize their taxes based on their financial situation. I'm always happy to help anyone interested, as I think that financial planning is a core skill that everyone needs, and one that allows people to work towards their goals and passions. There is more to financial planning than just budgeting, and I wanted to put together a resource that people could use as a guide for their financial journey. There are a lot of resources available that go into great depth, but I wanted to create a book that provided a foundation on numerous topics that are key to financial planning, investing, and tax optimization. If you consider yourself a financial genius, you will not find anything revolutionary in this book. It is intended for people looking for insights into concepts/ideas they have never heard of or lack context around. Being aware of these concepts will make you more prepared and able to "look around the bend" along your financial journey. I hope this book offers you insight and has a material impact on your life. Thank you for reading!

RESOURCES

I've centralized additional resources for chapters and sections in this book here: https://www.coreyganser.com/finance-book. I may edit/add to these resources over time to help provide additional insight and details.

WHY FINANCIAL PLAN?

When asked about why one should financial plan, I think about this quote from H. James Harrington: "Measurement is the first step that leads to control and eventually to improvement. If you can't measure something, you can't understand it. If you can't understand it, you can't control it. If you can't control it, you can't improve it." This is very true of financial planning. In order to plan and take control of your finances, you need to measure, set goals, and then identify improvements that will help you reach those goals. The one thing I want to stress is that no matter where you are at in your financial journey, it is never too late to start financial planning. Do not focus on lost time or opportunity, but instead set your sights on your goals and align your financial plan to support those goals.

Before we go any further, let's understand what constitutes a financial plan. Financial plans can be as simple as contributing monthly to a savings account to save up for a goal, but in this book we will cover multiple routes that you can take to organize your finances, benefit from investments, and gain an understanding of advanced financial strategies. This book will break down the concepts so that anyone can understand and implement them, and take them with them on their financial journey. I also include resources and links to further information on each of the advanced topics, so you can read more about them to help with your implementation.

GOALS

Goals, dreams, and life milestones get people thinking about financial planning. Identifying your goals and the financial requirements for accomplishing them is the first step to financial planning. A solid plan allows you to measure your progress and work towards achieving your goal. In this section I'll cover some common goals for people, and offer some tips for reaching them.

Vehicle

Buying/leasing a vehicle is a common goal. Depending on the distances you drive, the availability of other transportation options, and your budget, you have a lot of options.

Leasing a vehicle is one way to get a newer vehicle without a big upfront cost or loan. You don't own the vehicle, but instead are borrowing it and will have to return it at the end of the lease. Lease agreements include various terms that you have to comply with, including how many miles you can put on the vehicle. Make sure you evaluate in advance how much you typically drive, the efficiency of the vehicle you want, and your budget.

When buying a vehicle, the same is true. The benefit you gain from buying versus leasing is that you can hold onto the vehicle longer, and there are no restrictions on how you use it. This is similar to buying versus renting a home. You can change anything you want with the vehicle, and – unlike with a lease – you don't have to return it to its original state.

When buying, you have the option of buying new or used, which will depend on the vehicle specifications you want and your budget. Additional consideration should be given when looking at alternative fuel vehicles like electric vehicles (EVs), plug-in hybrid vehicles (PHEVs), hybrid vehicles, and fuel cell vehicles (FCVs). In most cases, incentives are available through your energy utility or city/state/federal government in the form of tax credits or rebates. While the upfront cost of such vehicles may be a little higher, the incentives can reduce the overall cost. I'll cover this a bit more in the tax section, but if you have the budget for an alternative fuel vehicle, I'd recommend talking with your accountant and seeing if this could help with your taxes.

Education

Educational goals – whether they involve gaining certifications, advanced degrees or licensures, or continuing professional development to maintain professional status – are unique in that they can also impact other financial goals. The most important thing about education is once you've gained knowledge, no one can take it away from you. It makes you more marketable and could increase your earning potential. Education can be very costly, so you need to identify what results you hope to gain from it. If you need a Master degree to continue in your field, research which institution offers a program that meets your requirements from a content and budget standpoint. If networking is important to your career path, and you've identified a university that is costly but hyper focused on your field, it may make more sense to invest in one of its programs than one from a more affordable school. At the end of the day, regardless of what institution you go to or what program you take, what you get out of education is directly tied to what you put in. The teachers/instructors will provide a foundation, but it is up to you to build on that foundation so that you can grow your knowledge and get a breadth of understanding in the topic. A single degree or certification program will not be all encompassing for the duration of your career. For example, while simply reading this book will help expand your financial literacy so you can achieve goals, I only cover the fundamentals. It's up to you leverage the addition resources I refer you and go deeper on topics that are important to you.

Home

You have most likely heard that the American dream is to own a home. While it isn't for everyone, owning a home is a great way to diversify your investments, save money, and have more control over your living situation. The affordability of a home – whether a house, townhome, condo, mobile home, tiny home, or other residence – will vary depending on the location, type of property and access to affordable interest rates. I will talk more about this in the chapter on real estate, but want to highlight a few reasons why owning your own home is appealing.

1. You can make it your own
   a. When you own your home, you can paint, update, and change pretty much anything you want (within the limits of any governing body, such as your city, state, or homeowners association). This is very appealing to some people, especially if they are coming from a living situation with many restrictions, such as renting.
2. It is typically cheaper than renting
   a. When you compare the cost of renting an equivalent property versus buying it, you'll find in most cases it is cheaper in the long run to buy than to rent. You'll need to make a down payment and pay closing fees, but monthly

mortgage costs (even with property tax and home insurance on top) are typically lower than rent. Note that this can vary depending on interest rates and the market you are looking at, but you should find it true in a lot of areas.

3. Your monthly 'rent' now builds equity

a. As you pay your mortgage, you are increasing the equity in your home. With the exception of interest-only loans, every mortgage payment will reduce the principal of the loan, or how much you still owe the bank before you completely own the property. You can also borrow against this equity in the future to support your other financial goals – a topic I will cover later in the section on borrowing against assets.

Most banks offer online calculators to help you evaluate what you can afford when buying a home. But ultimately, to estimate the monthly commitment you can afford to make, simply add the estimated monthly cost of the mortgage (principal plus interest) to the monthly costs for property tax and homeowners insurance. Property tax is typically paid every six months, so to calculate the monthly cost, take that payment and divide it by six. For homeowners insurance, your options will probably range from paying monthly to a whole year in advance, which is where you'll usually get the best deal. Evaluate what makes sense based on your finances, but you can use the monthly estimate for this calculation. I'll talk more about home ownership as a goal in the chapters on budgeting and real estate.

Retire early (FIRE)

A common goal in financial planning is to retire early. In fact, there is a movement, called FIRE (Financial independence, retire early), that focuses on that specific goal, and promotes some extreme measures for achieving it. A key to retiring early is making sure you properly define what retirement means. My definition of retirement is to stop doing what you have to do and start doing what you want to do. This is typically an underlying theme for any retiree. They want to travel more, spend more time with family, work on hobbies, or pursue a passion, to name a few. Instead of waiting for a specific age or financial marker, start identifying things in your life you can change now to help accomplish your retirement goals. The last thing you want to do when you retire is nothing. This leads to a sedentary lifestyle which isn't healthy. You want to stay active and have challenges for your mind and body. How this manifests in your life does depend on your goals and your age. The younger you are, the easier it is to pivot to a different industry for a career or to take risks, depending on your responsibilities. I encourage you to write down your definition of early retirement and then, for each item, identify how you could do it today. It may not look exactly as you had planned, but approaching your life with that mindset now will help you target the things that truly matter the most to you.

Minimalism

I've listed minimalism as a goal, but it is more of a lifestyle. You'll find a lot of overlap between the FIRE movement and minimalism. Minimalism is identifying what is most important in your life and removing distractions and frivolousness so you can focus on what matters. In the case of FIRE, this involves scaling back on extraneous spending, like eating out a lot or spontaneous purchases, and eliminating time-consuming activities that you aren't passionate about, so that what is left aligns with your true passions in life. I've called it out as a separate goal though, as it can help you achieve other financial goals and hone in on what truly matters. I'll include links in references for anyone interested to read more about minimalism.

Travel

The cost of travel can vary significantly, depending on where you want to go and how. One way to travel while also saving money is to find a job that incorporates it. This will allow you to visit different locations without having to pay for transportation and lodging. You may not be able to spend a lot of time at the location and you may want to return, but one nice thing about traveling with work is that you can typically build up frequent traveler points. This will then allow you to return to those locations, or other destinations, at a reduced cost, or even for free. If travel is a primary goal, then you may also want to consider looking at credit cards that offer travel rewards. I'll cover this more in the budgeting chapter.

Wedding

It's tempting to have a huge celebration when you marry, but you also want to make sure you start your new life together on a financially solid footing. Estimates of how much to spend on a wedding exist but, overall, I'd recommend evaluating what is comfortable for you and your partner. Make sure that it doesn't jeopardize any other goal or dreams that you have after the wedding, like buying a house, going on a trip, or other goals highlighted in this chapter. One question to ask yourself when you are planning a wedding is: will I remember this in 10 years? In the case of my own wedding, my wife and I had clear criteria as to what was critical for us. If any expense did not make it onto that list, we scrutinized it heavily to make sure it was meaningful enough to warrant the cost.

Family

Family is a broad goal and can mean many different things to each person. Some want more time with family, some want to have kids, some want to find someone to spend the rest of their life with, and so on. It is good to have a clear understanding of your family goals and to be aligned with your partner if you have one. If you plan to add kids, figure out how many and over what time period you want them. If you want to spend more time with family, what does that look like? While this doesn't have to be a task or milestone tracking goal, it is good to understand what you consider the minimum, so that you can do check-ins and make sure you are prioritizing your time to achieve your desired result. If your goal is to spend more time with your partner, but you find yourself preoccupied with a task that isn't as high a priority, make sure you pause and reflect and put more focus on your partner.

Other goals

You may see a trend in the goals that I've outlined. Before jumping into any goal, it is good to understand what success looks like and to also be pragmatic about what you need to accomplish that goal. Make sure you don't limit your future potential by over-allocating yourself in the present. This is true of financial commitments and time. Be prudent, but be aggressive to achieve your goals. Keep these goals in the forefront of your mind as you read the subsequent chapters to see how you can advance your goals with the materials I provide.

TRACKING/MEASURING

No matter what your goal is, you want to track and measure your progress towards it. This is especially important when you are setting financial goals. Besides setting up a budget, which we'll cover in the upcoming chapter, it is important to identify milestones and tasks that you can accomplish to get closer to your goals. This can involve writing down your goal on a piece of paper and highlighting all the individual tasks that you need to accomplish along with a reasonable timeline for accomplishing them. You can also use a project management tool that lets you assign tasks to yourself and see how much closer you are to achieving your goal as you check them off. Note that some goals – like that for family – can be hard to measure. In these instances, it is better to set daily reminders and reflect on what you can do that day to keep balance and achieve your goal. It could be a reminder to read stories to your kids before bed or to spend 15 minutes with your partner and provide moral support or a listening ear. Regardless of what your goals are, measuring will help remind you of steps you can take every day to get closer to your goal.

Managing others to achieve your goals

I'd like to call out another skill that is critical to achieving your goals. When you identify the tasks required to achieve your goals, you may notice there are some that you won't be able to do by yourself. In these instances, you'll most likely find someone that you can trust to help you complete these tasks. It is important to remember that this is your goal and that the person who is helping you will not be as committed to achieving your goal. This is 100% ok and common. To achieve your goal in the planned timeframe, make sure you manage the people you depend on. Managing them doesn't mean constantly nagging and checking in. Instead, I define it as holding them accountable for the commitments they make. I will typically ask someone when they can get a task completed and then set reminders for myself to check in with them as the deadline approaches. A lot of things can come up in a person's life that can distract them away from your task. They aren't necessarily ignoring it intentionally and usually it just takes a gentle reminder/check-in to make sure they are on track. If you have to routinely remind them and they continually miss deadlines, it may be time to identify a different person to complete those tasks. Your goal is really important, but don't get into the mindset of completing it at all costs. Treat everyone with respect, and be mindful that they have responsibilities outside of your tasks and that life can happen. Build flexibility into your timelines, but keep the flexibility to yourself, otherwise people will always use the time allotted.

BUDGETING

One of the first steps towards financial success is budgeting. This involves tracking and measuring your expenses and income so you can make calculated decisions that will impact your future. There are many tools available for budgeting, but I recommend a simple spreadsheet. I'll include a link in the references to a template that you can download and use for your own budgeting. At the most fundamental level, a budget should categorize your key areas of spending and track your estimated income for the upcoming year. This will allow you to see how much money you have left after covering all your expenses, as well as where you can cut back and adjust your priorities.

Managing a budget

Once you have your budget set up, I recommend reviewing it routinely and reconciling your expenses as they are paid. This will allow you to see how much money you have left over and whether there are any adjustments to make that will impact your future months. The template I've provided allows you to keep track of your current and anticipated balance, so that you can adjust your expenses if it looks set to enter negative territory.

When is credit good and when is it bad?

One of the easiest ways to fall behind financially is to carry debt that is high interest. Credit cards are the most notorious for having high interest rates that make repaying debt difficult. Instead of reducing the principal, you are continually paying off the accruing interest. If you are able to pay off your credit card every month, it becomes a tool in your financial planning arsenal that will benefit you. Almost every credit card has points or some type of rewards that accrue as you use it. By paying off your credit card every month, you don't have to pay interest and can then use the rewards as either a credit on your account or for things like gift cards and travel. If you tend to maintain a high balance, you'll need to change your behavior and make sure you only carry a balance that you can pay off when the bill is due.

Paying off expensive debt

As mentioned in the last section, credit cards can be a helpful tool in your financial plan, but they are also an example of really expensive debt that will make it hard for you to get ahead. The rule of thumb is to pay off any debt where the interest rate is higher than the return you could get investing that money. Now, this figure will depend on how much risk you are prepared to take when investing, but let's call it around 5%. If you have debt that is more expensive than that, you should consider paying it off instead of investing. This is a tricky area as mortgage rates can be over 6% and it is hard to pay mortgages off, so I'd focus on ranking your outstanding debt by interest rate and pay off any that is over 10%. When all your debt carries an interest rate of less than 10%, you can evaluate the effectiveness of your investments and see if you want to pay off more of the debt. It is also good to identify if there are any future changes to your debt, such as balloon payments (larger-than-usual one-off payments towards the end of a loan's term), that you need to factor in to assess the severity of any debt. As you pay off debt, you'll be in a better place to grow investments that will benefit you.

Leverage

Leveraging involves taking an asset that you have (such as your home or stocks) and borrowing against it so you can use that money for either other investing or expenses. Leveraging can be a useful addition to your financial toolkit, but must be approached with care. In upcoming chapters, you'll see how some very wealthy people use leverage to reduce their taxes and maximize their investments.

RISK

Before diving into all the ways you can save and invest money, I want to cover risk and how it will impact your strategy. Money can invoke a lot of emotion as it is associated with goals, dreams and wanting the best for the people we love. Identifying how comfortable you are with risk – or your 'risk appetite' – will help you align your money management strategy with your goals and personality.

Before you make any investment, it is critical that your financial advisor understands your risk appetite, so they will ask you questions, including about what you'd do in hypothetical situations.

For example:

You have a lot of shares in a company and the stock drops 10%. Please select your next action:

A. You immediately sell and look for a safer investment.

B. You hold your position and expect the stock to level out over time.

C. You buy more of the stock.

If you selected A, you tend towards being risk-averse and might do well to seek more stable investment options, albeit with lower returns. If you picked B, your risk appetite is average and you could probably handle typical market investments. If you went for C, you might be comfortable with riskier investments that could lose more money but offer potentially greater returns.

BANKING OPTIONS

The bank you use will have a big impact on your finances. It is strongly recommended to have three months' salary saved up in a stable savings account in case there is a drastic change in your life. Depending on your bank, interest rates on savings can be competitive (over 3% at the time of writing this) or not competitive at all (a consistent 0.10%). In some cases, you can also get a decent interest rate on the checking account you are using so you can truly make the most of money that you use to pay bills. Make sure you have checking and savings accounts that are easy to access and are maximized for their rate of return. Money market accounts are also useful and can offer competitive rates. I find though that rates in money markets are similar to those for competitive savings accounts, so your experience may be different depending on who you bank through.

Another offering from banks are certificates of deposit (CDs). These typically offer a fixed interest rate that doesn't change for the duration of the term, which can range from three months to beyond five years. Typically, the more you money put into these and the longer the term you choose, the higher the interest rate. Make sure you shop around on this too as I also see CD rates being close to those of competitive savings accounts. If you need easy access to your money, make sure you keep it in an account that allows this.

RETIREMENT

Planning for retirement usually represents a person's entry point into the world of investing. It can be hard, especially if you have immediate debt that you need to pay off. It is important, however, to maximize your retirement contribution so you have time to grow your retirement savings.

Social Security

Social Security is a federal program that takes money out of your paycheck and invests it to support people with a fixed income after retirement. The stability and longevity of the Social Security program is in question. Depending on your age, there is a chance that you may not receive a lot from Social Security, if anything at all. It is good to make sure you have enough savings in other retirement accounts to cover you just in case Social Security is gone before you retire. Assuming that Social Security is still around when you retire, there are some things you should consider as you get closer to retirement.

The first thing to note is that the Social Security payment is different for everyone. Social Security takes the highest 35 years of your earnings and then calculates the amount that is paid to you based on that. If you don't have 35 years of earnings, then your total social security payout will be impacted. There is a maximum benefit for Social Security, so even if you make a lot of money, yours will be capped at $3,345 per month at the time of writing this book.

Timing is also a key factor for Social Security. The earlier you retire, the less you will receive. There are a lot of nuances to Social Security and it is recommended you talk with your financial advisor once you are over the age of 50 and before you apply for Social Security.

Traditional and Roth IRA

To ensure you have enough when you retire, it is important to set up an account that is independent of Social Security, such as an individual retirement account (IRA). There are different types of IRAs, but the most common are 'traditional' and 'Roth'. Traditional IRAs allow you to add pre-taxed money to the retirement account. Depending on your tax-filing status, this could reduce your adjusted gross income (AGI) and lower your tax bill. You pay taxes on the money withdrawn from a traditional IRA when you retire. This could work to your benefit if you anticipate being in a lower tax bracket at retirement than your current tax bracket, but there is also the chance that tax rates will have increased by the time you retire, so you need to evaluate this option based on your current and anticipated tax situation. When you retire with a traditional IRA, there is also a required minimum distribution (RMD) – the minimum amount you must withdraw per year to eventually exhaust the funds in the account.

Roth IRAs are funded using after-tax money and the proceeds can be withdrawn tax free. The benefit of Roth IRAs is that the investments in the account can grow substantially, and when you retire you don't have to worry about paying taxes on the funds you withdraw. Note that with both traditional and Roth IRAs, the Internal Revenue Service (IRS) limits how much you can contribute per year. This can vary from year to year, so please check the current maximum on the IRS website or talk to an accountant. At time of writing, the maximum contribution is $6,500, or $7,500 if you are 50 or older. Note that there is no RMD with Roth IRAs. There are other requirements upon death, but overall you have more flexibility with the timing and amount of your withdrawals.

If you want to put more away for retirement, there are some options, but these will depend on your tax situation and the setup of your retirement accounts. To learn more, check out the sections on backdoor and mega backdoor IRAs. There are many retirement calculators out there that require you to estimate how much you want to put aside, how long you have until retirement, and your anticipated cost of living after retirement, etc. When you input this information, you may find the calculator predicts you will run out of money before your expected end of retirement. That is why it is important to start saving as early as you can and max out when possible, but also control your budget so you live within your means. This will allow you to go into retirement without a shock and will also make it easier to plan and understand how much money you'll need. Note that as you plan for retirement, there will be a change in your expenses. Most likely, things like mortgage costs will decrease or cease if you own your home, but costs for things like health insurance and food will increase with inflation. That is why when inflation is high and the stock market is volatile, it can be stressful for newly retired people as their source of income can decrease if the market falls while their costs can increase due to inflation. Make sure you talk with a financial advisor about this. As you get closer to retirement, also limit your exposure to risk and try to anticipate issues that could throw a wrench into the works.

401k and 403b

401k and 403b are other common retirement accounts you may have heard of. These are typically offered to employees through their employers. Contributions to 401k or 403b accounts can be pre-tax or post-tax and come directly out of your paycheck. When you leave a company, you will no longer be able to contribute to those accounts, but you can roll them over to a new employer's 401k/403b plan or roll over to a traditional IRA. Note that even though you can't contribute to them anymore, you will still be able to change the investments in the account and even actively invest if you are interested in doing that. 401k and 403b accounts are very similar to traditional IRAs and also have an RMD requirement upon retirement. These accounts have a higher annual contribution limit though, which is their main advantage compared to an IRA.

Rolling over retirement accounts

If you change jobs or end up opening multiple retirement accounts and want to consolidate them, you can roll over an account to the same type without being penalized. If you withdraw money from your retirement account and it doesn't count as a qualified distribution, you will be penalized and will have to pay a certain percentage of the amount to the government. To roll over, the accounts must be the same type, so check with both providers to verify this. Once you initiate the rollover, the old account will be closed and its balance will be credited to the new one. This can be a tricky process depending on the company that manages your retirement account, so consider seeking help from a financial advisor if you aren't comfortable.

Backdoor Roth IRA

Unlike traditional IRAs, Roth IRAs feature income limits that prohibit you from contributing if your annual income exceeds a certain amount (at the time of writing, your Modified Adjusted Gross Income must be under $129,000 for single tax filers). However, so-called backdoor Roth IRAs offer a way around this restriction. Essentially, you contribute to a traditional IRA (or account like a 401k) and then roll over to a Roth IRA so that those contributions can grow and be withdrawn tax free. Note that when you roll over to a Roth, you must pay taxes on any money in the traditional IRA that hasn't been taxed yet. This strategy is good for high-income individuals who will benefit from the tax-free growth offered by Roth accounts. This can get messy, especially with a Traditional IRA, so definitely consult an accountant to check whether a backdoor Roth account is the right option to optimize your current and future tax strategies.

Mega backdoor Roth IRA

If your employer has a 401k plan, and you are able to max it out but would still like to contribute more, the mega backdoor Roth could be an option. Mega backdoors aren't available to everyone though, as this depends on whether the administrator of your 401k plan supports the strategy. A mega backdoor Roth allows you to add after-tax dollars to your 401k and then convert it into a Roth. This allows the money to grow tax free. There can be a delay between the 401k contribution and the rollover, so you may end up owing a (usually small) amount of tax after the conversion, depending on whether the investments in the 401k grew between the time you contributed and it was converted to the Roth. Again, it's worth checking this with your accountant. The maximum amount you can contribute to retirement under a 401k while leveraging a mega backdoor is $61,000. This includes your pre-tax contribution ($20,500 at time of writing) along with any matching your employer may offer. When calculating your mega backdoor contributions, make sure you factor in the amount your employer will match, plus the timing of contributions, and ensure you don't exceed limits put in place by the IRS. This is a delicate balance to achieve, so it is good to verify how your employer matches contributions and also check with your accountant that you have balanced everything appropriately.

Converting traditional
to Roth

As mentioned, there are benefits to putting your money in a Roth account as it will grow tax free and you'll be able to withdraw tax free. If you have a traditional IRA account and you'd like to get the benefit of tax-free growth, you can convert it to a Roth. Doing this is a taxable event so you'll have to pay taxes on that amount transferred, but from that point forward you will not have to pay any more taxes on the money in the Roth account. This strategy works well during weak market conditions. Essentially, if you move your money to a Roth when the market is at or near its lowest point, you can then get the maximum benefit from tax-free gains when the market rebounds.

Matching

Some employers will match some or all of their employees' contributions to a retirement account. If yours does, try and take full advantage of it – it's essentially free money and allows you to grow your retirement account faster. Please check with your company's human resources department to see if it offers contribution matching and find out how you can maximize the benefits.

EDUCATION SAVINGS ACCOUNT (ESA)

An education savings account (ESA) is an investment account where you pay in after-tax dollars that then grow tax free and can be withdrawn tax free to cover qualifying education expenses. These are typically set up for children so that they will have money for college. However, depending on the ESA you choose, the funds can also be used for K-12 education. There are two primary ESA accounts: Coverdell and 529. One key difference between the two is that parents who earn over a certain amount (at time of writing, $110,000 annual income for single filers and $220,000 for married couples filing jointly) are not allowed to contribute to a Coverdell. Also, the maximum that can be contributed to a Coverdell is $2,000 per year. Contributions to a 529 are assumed to fall under the gift tax exemption, which at time of writing was set at $16,000 per year with a lifetime limit of $12.92 million. There are no income limits for contributing to a 529 account. Depending on what state you live in, you may also get benefits from the 529 on your state taxes.

Regardless of which plan you select, saving for the minor in your life is a great way to ensure that graduating from college has less of an impact on their future finances. Note that with the 529, you are unable to choose the investments, but with Coverdell you have more flexibility. To identify which account type is most advantageous for your education savings and taxes, talk with your accountant and compare their limitations.

HEALTH INSURANCE

Health insurance is a key part of your financial plan. You want to ensure that costs not covered by your insurance don't have a negative impact on your finances if you need to use it. There are a lot of things to evaluate with health insurance, but here are a few suggestions to help with your decision-making:

1. Check what services are covered. It's important to identify worst-case scenarios for your and your family's health.

2. Look at which providers (doctors, clinics, therapists, etc) are 'in network'. These are providers with whom the insurance company has negotiated rates, meaning coverage costs them – and ultimately you – less money.

3. Review the deductible to see how much you'll have to pay before the insurance plan starts covering more. Certain services (such as a physical or specific shots) are usually included for free, but for other services a co-pay (per-visit fee) will apply. Check how much you are expected to pay and whether you have that money saved up in case of emergency.

4. Make sure you know your plan's out

of pocket maximum – essentially, the maximum amount you will have to pay for covered services in a plan year after you've reached your deductible – and have the ability to cover it in case of emergencies. Once the out-of-pocket max threshold is hit, the insurance plan will cover 100% of the services that they cover. It is also good to identify which services still aren't covered (see bullet point 1) even if you hit your out-of-pocket max.

5. There are high deductible health plans (HDHP) where the deductible is high, but you can have and contribute to a health savings account (HSA). With an HSA you can contribute pre-tax dollars that can be used to pay for health expenses directly or be reimbursed if you covered the expenses with separate funds.

    1. HSAs also offer tax benefits. Contributing pre-tax dollars lowers your adjusted gross income (AGI). You can also withdraw from an HSA as reimbursement for a qualifying medical expense. Depending on your tax bracket, this can help reduce taxes you owe at the end of the year. If you are a high earner, definitely talk to your advisor about the benefits of an HSA.

2. Some HSA providers also allow you to invest your HSA funds, which then grow tax free and can be withdrawn tax free for qualifying medical expenses. If you don't have a lot of immediate medical expenses, they can act as another investment vehicle that will benefit you in the future.

INVESTING OUTSIDE OF
RETIREMENT AND EDUCATION

Next, I will dig into investing outside of retirement. The upcoming chapters will cover types of investment that you may have heard of or are familiar with, and some investment types that will be completely new to you. A key aspect to investing is to diversify so that you don't have all your assets in one specific investment type or even in one specific stock. I will also cover some concepts in the chapters on brokerages and trading to help you evaluate investment options for your retirement accounts. As stressed throughout this book, none of this information I share constitutes financial or legal advice, and you should talk to a professional before proceeding with any changes to your investment or tax strategies.

BROKERAGES

Brokerages are businesses that facilitate the buying and selling of items between parties. In this part of the book, we will focus on their role in trading securities like stocks. Some common brokerages include TD Ameritrade, eTrade, and Robinhood, to name a few. Most big banks have a brokerage arm as well. Before the internet, if you wanted to buy a stock, you were required to go through a broker – a person who works at a brokerage. That person would take your money and try to buy the stock you wanted. Nowadays, you still have to go through a brokerage, but the internet has digitized the process so that you can buy/sell through a website or application without having to interact with a specific person. We have even reached the point where transactions can be programmatically initiated, which I'll cover under the section on algorithm trading.

FUNDS

Before getting into trading, I want to highlight some of the common funds that people and retirement accounts invest in. At the most simplistic level, a fund is a collection of securities grouped together under a common theme/goal. There are multiple classifications for funds, but in this chapter I will cover the following: mutual funds, exchange traded funds (ETFs), index funds, and hedge funds.

Mutual funds

Mutual funds have been around for a while and are typically what people have in mind when they hear the word 'fund'. They allow investors to diversify their risk across multiple securities grouped under a specific theme. For example, some mutual funds have a tech theme that stipulates all securities invested in are related to technology companies. The fund's theme can be segmented even further, such as by focusing on 'large cap' (companies whose total issued shares have a high value – over $25 million) or 'small cap'. Mutual funds are managed by people who are typically called fund managers. These individuals make sure that the group of securities in the fund offer the best return while also staying in line with the fund's theme/intent. When reviewing mutual funds, first check that the return they offer is competitive and in alignment with your financial goals. Mutual funds also charge investors a fee that is used to pay the fund managers for their active management of investments. Pay attention to this when selecting a mutual fund, as some funds charge high fees that reduce your returns. Typically, these fees are reflected in the fund's 'expense ratio', which shows the percentage of your total investment that is paid to the fund manager. Ultimately, the lower the expense ratio, the more of your investment returns you get to keep.

Exchange traded funds (ETFs)

An exchange traded fund, also known as an ETF, is similar to a mutual fund in that its value is based on a group of securities that share a specific theme. However, unlike with a mutual fund, it doesn't actually own the securities – it simply tracks them. One of the big differences between a mutual fund and an ETF is that ETFs can be traded like stocks throughout the day on the market. A mutual fund can only be traded at the end of the day and that is when buy/sell transactions occur. ETFs typically charge lower fees than mutual funds, which is an attractive proposition for investors looking for diversification and to also reduce their expense ratio.

Hedge funds

Hedge funds are typically more aggressive than ETFs or mutual funds. The fund manager can also choose to invest in assets that are not securities, such as real estate, currencies and other alternative investments (see the chapter on alternative investments to learn more). They use leverage and options to help hedge their bets while increasing their returns. To invest in a hedge fund, investors must be accredited. Historically, this meant they had a net worth of over $1 million and had earned over $200,000 a year for at least the previous two years, although increasing emphasis is also now being placed on investors' educational backgrounds.

TRADING

Trading is the buying and selling of assets like securities with the intention of making a profit. This has traditionally been done through the manager of a brokerage, who buys/sells investments on your behalf and deals with another broker on the other side of the transaction. These are the people you see yelling and waving in the air in the traditional image of a trading floor. This is how the stock market – essentially, a group of exchanges – worked when it was first established. Some popular exchanges in the United States include the New York Stock Exchange (NYSE) and the Nasdaq. Over time, and with advances in technology, such transactions have come to require less manual intervention, and most buys and sells are now handled by computers. There is still a buyer and a seller, but the actual transaction and sale is mostly automated.

Opportunity cost

With any purchase or investment, it is important to make sure you are maximizing the potential of your money. To do this, you have to understand its opportunity cost – essentially, what you could miss out on if the money were used in a different way. As an example, let's say you want to buy a used car that costs $15,000, but already have a car that works. If you chose instead to invest the $15,000, you would have the opportunity of making a financial return on the investment. Let's call it $750, based on a theoretical 5% annual return. If you chose to buy the car, the opportunity cost would be that $750 potential investment income that you missed out on. When comparing investments, you should also understand the estimated term of the investment. In the case of securities like certificates of deposit (CDs), you commit to not receiving back your money for a specific time period, unless you pay a penalty. The opportunity cost in this instance is the other needs you could have fulfilled by using that money while it was locked up in the CD. The needs could be personal purchases or investments. When evaluating investments, it is good to ask yourself if you'll need the money in the next three to six months. If you do, then evaluate which investments would provide the most liquidity so you can withdraw it at any time without being penalized, while also ensuring the investment isn't so risky that you could lose the amount you'll need.

Basics of trading

I want to dig into trading a little bit more but will provide resources where you can go into greater detail. When you buy a security, you typically have the option to specify the price you want to pay for it. If you have a specific amount of money and want to make sure you can buy a certain number of shares, you can set a limit order. A limit order allows you to specify the maximum price you want to buy a security for, and you can set an expiration for how long that limit is available. For example, let's say you want to buy 100 shares of ACME company for $10 and this limit order will stay intact for the next 90 days. If the ACME company stock is trading at $10.64, your order will not execute. As soon as it gets to $10 or below, the limit order will trigger and the broker will try and find a seller that matches your requirements. The same is true when you are looking to sell. If you don't need to achieve a specific price for the share, you can also buy/sell at market price (the average price the stock is buying/selling for) and the broker will then work on matching your request to the next available party.

I want to take a quick detour and call out something that isn't very clear when you are trading securities, but which makes sense when you realize how it works. If you are looking to buy securities and no one is looking to sell, your trade will not execute even if the stock is valued for your limit price or even if you do a market order. This is also true of selling. It may seem obvious, but it is easy to gloss over this, especially if you start with trading big name stocks/securities and then start trading more obscure securities (see the upcoming section on the pink sheet market). It's a good idea to seek advice from your financial advisor when you're unsure how easy or difficult it might be to buy/sell a specific security. To gain a better understanding of the likelihood that trades will execute, read the section on technical analysis.

Paper trading

Trading may seem overwhelming when you are getting started, but the good news is that there are ways to practice without losing money. When you start off with any type of securities trading, you can usually sign up for a paper account. A paper account allows you to try out different trading strategies with fake money. It uses real market data so that you can test trading hypotheses and even try out day trading. Before you make risky trades, I'd recommend paper trading for a while so that you can see when the market works for you and against you.

Fundamental analysis
vs technical analysis

When evaluating stocks for trading, there are two primary types of research traders use: fundamental analysis and technical analysis. They both offer different insights into the stock's behavior and that of the company behind it.

We'll start with fundamental analysis. One of the most well-known investors is Warren Buffett. He has an impressive background and I recommend reading a biography on him. But to cut to the core of his success, he mostly relies on fundamental analysis to understand the inner workings of companies he wants to invest in. Fundamental analysis involves examining all the financial information about a company and seeking to understand its operations. When a company is traded on a primary market, it is required by the Securities and Exchange Commission (SEC) to publish information about its operational and financial performance. This information helps you build a deeper understanding about the company, including how successful its products and services are, whether it is making a profit or loss, and what its projected growth is. Fundamental analysis requires building some skills, including how to read the reports that companies release. It can also be very time consuming, and this can lead to 'analysis paralysis', where you are so stuck in the data that you have a hard time making a decision. With that in mind, here are some tips for how to approach fundamental analysis:

1. When picking companies to research, make sure you start with ones that operate in an industry that you are most familiar with. This will allow you to understand their overall business better and cut to the key metrics that show you whether they are successful.

2. Fundamental analysis is great if you are trying to pick a few winning stocks, but if you diversify your investments into funds, there is less of a need for it as your risk is already distributed across multiple stocks. Just make sure the fund you invest in has enough diversity and aligns with the investment goals that you've identified with your financial planner.

3. Recommendations from analysts that also use fundamental analysis can be helpful, but take their feedback with a grain of salt. Analysts have their own biases and interpretations, so gaining an understanding of their perspective might be useful, but at the end of the day it is your money and you need to understand the companies you are investing in.

Technical analysis is more focused on the

movement, history, and trajectory of a stock itself. It involves looking at how many trades occur in the stock and where there is resistance to movements in its price, as well as other metrics that help traders understand when they should buy and sell. Technical analysis is more popular with day traders, as they rely on real-time movements in stocks to make a profit. Both of these areas are complex and I won't delve into them too deeply here, but you can review the resources I provide to learn more.

Bots and algorithm trading

In the last section, I mentioned that a lot of trading has been conducted automatically for some time. This has introduced a new era in trading, in which trades are initiated based on programmatic triggers. This means a person can set up a program to check for certain market conditions or specific thresholds for a stock. If these are found, the program will automatically buy and sell without manual intervention. This is known as algorithm trading or trading with bots, because the programs run pretty autonomously and triggers are typically based on algorithms. Most large financial firms use bots as a way to manage their investments and rebalance them if there is a change in market conditions. During the past couple of years though, there has been an increase in the activity of so-called retail traders, which has had a dramatic impact on markets. Retail traders are regular people (rather than the employees of financial firms) who manually trade through apps or brokerage sites and usually don't take a programmatic approach. The popularity of 'meme stocks' – stocks that gain a huge social following, with retail traders generating or following online recommendations that may contradict conventional trading wisdom – has caused huge swings in stock prices. In some cases, this has caused professional traders to lose a good amount of money. I'll talk about this a bit more in the section on short selling.

Pink sheet market

The lesser-known pink sheet market comprises companies that aren't listed on major stock exchanges like the NYSE or Nasdaq and which therefore are not subject to such strict financial reporting requirements. Many are so-called penny stocks, which trade at under $5 per share. These can be very small companies that are working hard to grow and don't have the financial resources to be listed on one of the main exchanges but still want the benefit of being listed for fundraising. Definitely talk with your financial advisor/broker if you are interested in penny stocks. Trading them can be high risk but, as with a lot of things in investing, higher risk can also mean higher reward.

Short selling

So far, I've covered buying and selling securities with the intention of making money when the underlying security increases in value. However, if you suspect that a security is going to go down in value, you can also 'short' it. This involves borrowing the security, selling it and then buying it back for less money when its price has dropped. The difference in price between when you sold it and bought it back is your profit. Shorting securities is very risky and can generate greater losses than owning a security. To highlight the risk involved, here's an example.

Let's say you short ACME's stock when its current market price is $10 per share. You suspect that the price will drop to $8 and that you'll be able to pocket the $2 per share difference. If you owned the ACME stock and the company went out of business, you would lose $10 multiplied by the number of shares you own. If you shorted the stock and ACME rallied to $30 per share, you would be down $20 per share, which is the difference between its original market price and the new share price. This doesn't mean that you would immediately have to come up with that money, but if you suspect that the stock is going to continue climbing, you'll want to cut your losses and drop your position. In order to close your short position, you'll have to buy the stock at the market price of $30 per share. If there is a lot of short interest in the stock, a so-called short squeeze can occur. This happens when the price of an underlying security that has had a lot of short interest jumps rapidly and short positions are closed as traders seek to reduce their losses. In order to close their short positions they need to buy the security, which in turn creates more demand for the security and can continue to drive up its price. This is a classic example of supply and demand. When demand is high and supply is short, the price of the goods will increase. You may have seen examples of this during 2020 and 2021 with meme stocks like AMC or GameStop. There was a lot of retail investor interest in these stocks, which drove up their price, and the number of short positions in the market then caused the price to skyrocket. This can be exacerbated by advanced traders' use of bots, which automatically close short positions if a price limit is hit. This automated triggering can cause a tidal wave of action across a bunch of securities or even the market as a whole.

If you are interested in short selling, I strongly recommend discussing it with your financial advisor or broker and seeking to truly understand all its associated risks.

Dividends

Dividends are cash payments that a company makes to shareholders if they have generated enough profit in the quarter or year. Not all companies pay dividends, and the frequency of the payment can vary, with a company perhaps paying a dividend one year but nothing the next. Some companies, such as real estate investment trusts (REITs), are required to pay a dividend, but the frequency of that dividend will depend on the company. You can read more about REITs in the real estate section. Dividends are counted as taxable profits for traders and investors, and you can use the money to buy other securities or you can reinvest it back in the original stock. If your brokerage supports a dividend reinvestment plan (DRIP), it will automatically buy shares in the stock that issued the dividend when it is paid. If you like to track your return on investment closely, I'd recommend tracking these transactions as reinvesting profit works similarly to compounding interest.

Capital gains

Capital gains are the profits you make when you sell or exit an investment. There are two main types: short-term capital gains and long-term capital gains. Short-term capital gains occur when you hold a security for less than a year and make a profit from it. Long-term capital gains occur when you hold onto a security for longer than a year.

Both types of capital gains are taxable, but rates are usually higher for short-term than long-term gains, depending on your tax bracket. In both cases, if you sell the security and lose money, you aren't taxed on that – and in fact, the loss will be carried into your net investment income calculation so could reduce the amount of tax you pay overall. Be mindful that a big capital gains profit could push you into a higher tax bracket. Capital gains will be covered more in the upcoming chapters on tax, bonds and real estate, as there are ways to reduce or delay their tax impact. For example, if you want to be a more active trader and not have to worry as much about the impact on your adjusted gross income and taxes, I'd recommend using one of your retirement accounts, as any profits will be either taxed later, in the case of a traditional IRA, or not taxed, in the case of a Roth IRA.

As always, please review this with your financial advisor and accountant to understand the impact on your investments and your taxes before changing anything.

Margin accounts

When you have an investment account, some brokerages will allow you to also use it as a margin account. A margin account allows you to borrow money, using your investments as collateral, at a specific interest rate. When you do this, you are essentially taking out a loan from the brokerage without having to go through the background and credit checks associated with car or home loans. As with any other loan, you have to pay it back. And depending on the value of your investments, a so-called margin call may occur where the collateral of your investments isn't enough to cover the margin loan and the brokerage will require you to deposit more money or buy more securities to keep it in good standing. Depending on the brokerage, you can use the loan money to invest or, in some cases, withdraw and use for things unrelated to investing. I'll talk more about margin accounts in the tax section, but using a margin account is a higher-risk activity and you should review this with your financial advisor before even asking for it to be enabled on an account.

Employee stock purchase programs

Employee stock purchase programs allow employees of a company that has tradable stock to buy that stock at a discount. There is typically an open period during which the employee can enroll in the program and have money withheld from their paycheck to buy the stock at a discount. If you have confidence in the company you work for and have the available funds to do this, it is a great way to build wealth. The discount you receive is also essentially free money. You could sell the stock right away and, assuming the stock hasn't suddenly dropped dramatically, take that discount as a profit (the difference between the price you bought it at and the market price you sell it at). If your company offers an employee stock purchase program, review it with your financial advisor and accountant and see if it makes sense for you.

Restricted stock units (RSUs)

Restricted stock units (RSUs) are stock awards that are given to employees who work at companies with a tradable stock. They are a bit like bonuses. As soon as you receive the stocks, you can sell them and use the money to buy other investments or something unrelated. There typically isn't an opt-in requirement as this is money the company is giving to you. There is typically a vesting schedule, which means you receive portions of the RSUs at fixed intervals over a set period of time, such as every six months or once a year. For example, if you are granted 120 RSUs over a vesting period of four years and it vests every six months, the 120 shares will be divided into eight payouts, each of 15 shares. Note that typically taxes are withheld, so the amount deposited into your brokerage account may be reduced depending on how much tax is due. If you work at a company that grants RSUs, definitely talk with your financial advisor and accountant about how best to use them.

Options

An option essentially gives the holder the option to buy or sell an associated security at a specified price. Options are used for multiple purposes, which I'll touch on a bit in this chapter. Options are fairly complex though, so review the references I provide to learn more about them.

My first experience with options came when I was working at a startup that offered stock options as part of its employees' compensation. With startups, stock options give you the right to buy stock at a specified price called a strike price. As with RSUs, such options typically have a vesting schedule. This allows you to buy more shares the longer you are at the company. You typically don't execute your right to buy until an exit event happens, such as you leaving the company or the company being acquired. You then pay the strike price times the number of shares that have vested and are allowed to be purchased. You then own the stock and can sell it when you are able to. Startup options are however one of the least common types of option and are not typically accessible to the average investor.

Options on the stock market are more common. These give you the option to buy or sell the underlying security at a specified price. The interesting thing about options is that the option itself can increase or decrease in value based upon movements in the underlying stock. This means that you can buy/sell/short the option contract itself, just like you could the underlying security. To get an option you have to pay what is called a premium. Each option represents 100 units of the underlying security. Here's an example:

There is an option contract for ACME company with a strike price of $10. As a reminder, the strike price is the amount you'd pay if you execute the option. The option has an expiration date three months from now and the premium on the contract is $1.30. In order to acquire this option contract for ACME, you would pay $130 (the premium multiplied by 100, which is the number of shares represented by each option contract). Let's say the ACME stock jumps to $11 and the premium for your contract rises to $1.80 (there is some correlation between the stock price and the premium, but there are lots of other factors that come into play so it isn't 1:1). If you sell your options contract, you'll get back $180, which would be a $50 profit over your initial investment, or about a 38% return. If you had bought the 100 shares of ACME instead of the option, you would have had to pay $1,000 ($10/share x 100 shares) and when you sold it, you would have received $100. That would represent only a 10% return on investment ($100 return / $1,000 to purchase the shares). Therefore, the option would return a higher percentage with less upfront investment. You could also execute your option contract and buy 100 shares of ACME for $10 per share. If you didn't buy the shares and didn't sell the contract and your option expired, then you would lose the $130 premium you paid to buy the options contract.

Options can also be used as a kind of insurance policy for investment portfolios. Imagine that you have 1,000 shares in ACME that you bought for $10 per share. The stock looks solid and has been slowly increasing, but you suspect there may be some volatility coming up and you want to be able to liquidate your shares if the market takes a turn for the worse. You can purchase an options contract that allows you to sell your 1,000 shares at a specified price where you still make a profit or minimize the loss. Financial firms like hedge funds do something similar to allow them to make riskier bets while minimizing losses. They may lose the premium for the options contract, but this is a small price to pay to avoid potentially much bigger losses in the underlying investment as well as losing the confidence of their clients.

As I mentioned above, options are fairly complex and I've only scratched the surface in this section. You can read more about them in the resources I provide.

Bonds

Bonds are essentially loans where you are the entity that is lending the money. Typically, companies or governments issue bonds to raise money for a specific project or purpose and commit to repaying the principal back after a specified period of time, plus an agreed interest rate. Bonds are typically seen as safer investments than securities like stocks, but they still carry risk, which is tied to the company or government that is issuing the bond. As with individuals, companies and governments have their own credit rating that reflects their likely ability to repay debts. If they have a really bad credit rating, there is higher risk that buyers of the bond will not be paid back completely, but typically the interest rate on the bond is set higher to compensate for this risk.

There are multiple types of bonds. Bonds issued by companies are typically called corporate bonds. The federal government can issue bonds and so can the Treasury department. For example, the savings bonds that used to be given at birthdays are Treasury bonds, which are typically considered very low risk. One of the more popular Treasury bonds in recent years is the Series I bond, whose interest rate rises or falls broadly in line with inflation. This investment option therefore helps people partly offset rises in inflation, which during 2022 was quite high.

Municipal bonds, also called munis, are issued by local governments and are typically used to fund projects within the community. Any interest that you receive from municipal bonds is usually exempt from federal income tax and may also be exempt from local and state taxes, depending on the state where you live. If you are looking to diversify your portfolio or to stabilize it a bit more, definitely talk to a financial advisor and accountant about how you might use bonds to help.

REAL ESTATE INVESTING

Real estate investing is another way to diversify your investments. The most common real estate investment is purchasing a primary home to live in. This could be a single-family home, townhome or condo, etc. When you purchase the property, you are buying an asset that might appreciate over time. The asset that you are building equity in can also be leveraged in the future by borrowing against it. When buying a principal residence, you will most likely need to get a mortgage – a loan that will allow you to buy the property and make monthly repayments. There are different types of mortgages available, depending on factors like how much money you have to put down as a deposit, your credit score, and the price of the property you are buying. Here are a few of the common types:

- Federal Housing Administration (FHA) loan – This is provided through the United States Department of Housing and Urban Development (HUD). FHA loans are more flexible than conventional mortgages. They allow you to make smaller down payments, have lower closing costs and have less strict credit score requirements. Typically, the interest rate is higher and you will most likely also have to pay for private mortgage insurance (PMI). This is an additional cost added to loans when the down payment/equity is less than 20%. In some cases, if your property increases in value so that your equity rises to 20% of the loan or greater, you can remove the PMI, but be sure to verify this. Make sure you talk with your bank to identify if an FHA loan is a good option for you.

• Veterans Affairs (VA) loan – This is offered to veterans or currently enlisted members of United States military branches. The benefits of VA loans are similar to those of FHAs, but you don't need to pay PMI. If you are a service member or veteran, definitely check with your bank and see if a VA loan is a good fit for you.

• Conventional loan – Unlike an FHA or VA, this isn't guaranteed by the government so usually doesn't have as much flexibility on credit score requirements or reduced closing costs. You also typically need a bigger down payment for conventional mortgages, because the lending institution is taking more risk since the loan isn't guaranteed by the government. You'll often get better rates with a conventional loan, but it depends on the market. Again, check with your bank to identify the best loan option for you.

There are sub-categories within these types of home loans based on the structure of the payback and interest rates. The two most common sub-categories are fixed-rate mortgages and adjustable-rate mortgages (ARMs). With a fixed-rate mortgage you have the same interest rate for the loan's duration, which is most commonly 15, 20 or 30 years. Adjustable-rate mortgages have a fixed rate for a set initial period of the loan, after which it becomes adjustable, meaning that it moves up or down in line with movements in interest rates set by the central bank. ARMs are appealing as you can typically get a lower initial interest rate than with a fixed-rate mortgage. However, at the end of the adjustable period – which typically runs for five, seven or 10 years – you face the risk that rates may rise quickly.

With both types, you always have the option to refinance if broader interest rates drop enough to make it worthwhile. To figure out if this is the case, work out how many months it would take before you break even on the refinancing costs. First, figure out how much you would save in mortgage repayments per month and then divide the closing costs by that amount.

For example, let's say you got a loan of $150,000 and had an interest rate of 7%. Your monthly payment would be around $998. Let's say that interest rates dropped to 5%. This would reduce your monthly payment to around $805. This means you'd save $193/month. If the closing costs for refinancing were $2,000, you'd need to stay in that property for around 10 or 11 months for the refinancing to be worth it ($2,000 closing cost / $193 savings per month = 10 1/3 months). If you know you will be in the house for that long or more, it may be worth refinancing.

If refinancing doesn't make financial sense but you are looking for a way to reduce your monthly payment, check with your loan provider to see if they allow recasting of your mortgage. This involves you putting more money down to reduce the principal and the bank then readjusting the mortgage payment to reflect this but with the same loan duration. Typically, you need a larger amount of money to do this, so check with your bank to see if they support it and what the requirements are. Also, the bank may charge a recasting fee, but it should be small in comparison to refinance closing costs.

If you are considering either refinancing or recasting, always check with your financial planner and bank first to see if doing so makes sense.

Vacation/secondary home

You may find yourself in a position where you could buy a vacation home or secondary home. This is one way for you to increase your real estate investment without having to transition to being a landlord. Your reason for buying a vacation home could be a desire to be near family, it could be connected to work travel or you might simply like to take regular breaks in a particular place.

Having a vacation/secondary home requires a lot of careful consideration. Ask yourself the following questions and if you can't say yes to all of them, talk through the concerns and make sure you are prepared:

• Are you able to afford the mortgage and associated costs without a change in your income?

• Are there any career changes coming up that could affect your ability to afford it?

• Are you ok with leaving it vacant for multiple months and in some cases longer if you can't get there?

• Are you buying in a location where you anticipate property prices will appreciate over time?

• Are there people or service providers who you trust to watch/fix things at the property?

If you can say yes to all of these or even have a plan where you say no, then it may make sense to explore buying a vacation/secondary home. I'd recommend talking with a realtor and your financial advisor to make sure this aligns with your short-term and longer-term financial plan and that it is a good time to proceed.

Rental

If you like the prospect of being a landlord and making money from investment properties, you may want to consider buying a rental. There are various types of rental property, including single family homes, condos, townhomes, office buildings, and other commercial properties. To buy a rental, make sure you have the financing for it. If you need a loan, you'll have to talk to the bank, which will typically charge you higher interest rates for a rental property than for a primary or vacation/secondary property. This is typically because buying a rental property exposes lenders to more risk, such as your ability to find tenants that are able to cover the mortgage. Before proceeding with the purchase of a rental, I definitely encourage you to do more research – check out the resources as some starting points.

Here are some things to consider:

• Are you able to afford the mortgage payments if you can't find tenants?

• Based on rents for comparable rental properties in the market, will you be able to make a profit from the rental?

• Are you going to fix any issues at the rental property yourself, or do you have trusted service providers who can perform the repairs?

• What are the laws for rentals in the area where you

are buying?

- Do you know how to advertise and find tenants for your property?

- Will you set up a business for the rental? (See more information about setting up a business later in this book.)

- Will you allow pets at your rental?

Being a landlord can be profitable depending on the properties you buy and the rental market. I've been a landlord for over 10 years and one of my key recommendations is to look at the property and the setup and ask yourself if you'd rent it. If you wouldn't, then review what changes would be needed for you to want to live there. Not all landlords approach rentals with this mentality, but I've found keeping my property in good condition, and possibly offering some small extras, make the property more marketable and my tenants more respectful of it.

Furnished rentals are more costly for landlords but can also be more profitable. Whether you are listing a furnished rental on Airbnb or on websites that support corporate housing, you can typically charge more, but you also have the cost of providing furnishings and getting them cleaned when tenants move out. The high tenant turnover associated with sites like Airbnb raises your costs further, as you need to pay for frequent cleaning as well as oversight to ensure people check in and out on time. As with regular rentals, you need to evaluate different locations to ensure there is enough interest in furnished rentals there to warrant the investment.

Real estate syndication

Real estate syndication is another way to invest in real estate while reducing the burden of day-to-day property management. Here, you provide money in exchange for a share of the ownership of one or multiple properties. The person who organizes the deal is responsible for management of the properties and typically sets up a business to formalize the structure. Through this business, investors receive income and, in some cases, tax benefits that are similar to those if you owned the property directly. Make sure that you review the structure of the syndication carefully and consult a lawyer and other trusted advisors to ensure you are protected. Real estate syndications may require you to be an accredited investor, so verify that you are able to meet their requirements before spending time or resources.

Real estate investment trust (REIT)

If you like the idea of real estate investing but don't want to deal with the maintenance of the property or don't want to be a landlord, you can invest in a real estate investment trust (REIT, pronounced 'Reet'). A REIT is a trust that invests in different real estate and collects money through rent. The properties could be residential or commercial. You can buy shares in REITs, which are usually available on the stock market. By law, REITs must pay out regular profits to their shareholders as dividends. This is usually quarterly, but some REITs pay monthly. Investing in a REIT can allow you to further diversify your investments into real estate without the upfront cost and effort associated with being a landlord.

Real estate tax benefits

There are multiple tax benefits available from real estate, but this ultimately depends on your tax situation and the type of real estate investing you do. Instead of covering it in this section, I've included information on real estate tax benefits in the chapter on tax strategies so you can view them alongside other options.

ALTERNATIVE INVESTMENTS

Alternative investments are investments that lie outside the world of traditional financial assets like stocks or bonds – and I bet you've already had experience with them. If you've ever had a collection of any type, that could be considered an alternative investment. For example, trading cards, toys and cars are all assets with some associated value that you may be able to extract in the future by selling them. I'll list below some non-typical alternative investments that you may have heard of through media or online references or have just wondered about. This isn't intended to be exhaustive, and I encourage you to do additional research if one of these topics sticks out to you as interesting.

- Art – This has always attracted interest as an investment option. The internet has made art more accessible and increased exposure for new artists who are less known but have strong messages within their art. Art is very subjective as an investment so if you are interested in it, I encourage you to establish a strategy that aligns with your goals. If you appreciate art, want to support artists and are looking for pieces to decorate your home, you can still consider these investments and you can do research to align with your goals. Note that if you are strictly looking to maximize your investment and do not care as much for the art's messaging, that will require a different approach and possibly involve acquiring the work of more widely known artists. Either way, make sure you understand the risks of investing in art, including the chance that value is lost if an art piece is damaged.

- Music – With the growth of streaming services, music has turned into a very lucrative industry. Previously, a person could buy a CD and listen non-stop. With streaming, artists and the owners of music rights are paid every time someone listens to a track. Not only does this extend the profits from music, it also provides valuable insight for artists as to which tracks their fans love the most. Investors have started buying the rights to music so they can receive royalties when the music is played. This is a bit more complex than buying a piece of art, but it is increasingly popular. Another option is to pull out your instrument and create music yourself. I'll cover this more in a future chapter. If you are interested in purchasing the rights to music, do some research around specific firms that can arrange this transaction for you.

- Intellectual Property – Almost every industry has patents or trademarks that protect intellectual property, essentially to prevent inventions from being copied. Investors can buy rights to patents and receive royalties from them through the sale of associated products. For example, if you bought the patent to a lotion, you would receive royalties for every unit of that lotion that was sold. There are a lot of gray areas in this space so if you are considering investing make sure you hire a lawyer to review the scope of the intellectual property and that you have a clear path to return on your investment.

• Cryptocurrency – Also called crypto, this has been a popular, and in some cases controversial, investment. Cryptocurrency is a digital currency that is recorded on a blockchain and which can be used to buy things online or in person if the business accepts it. A lot of people invest in cryptocurrency, as its price can move around a lot, which allows them to buy/sell it and sometimes make a profit. Investing in crypto is similar to investing in traditional currencies like the United States dollar or the euro, but cryptocurrency has historically been more volatile, meaning prices can experience much bigger increases and falls. Cryptocurrencies you may have heard of include Bitcoin, Ethereum and Dogecoin, but there are numerous others out there. Recently there have been some notable failures, such as FTX, that have caused people to lose money. As with any investment, there is risk with cryptocurrency and you need to evaluate that risk and weigh it out. If you are interested in investing in cryptocurrency, there are some brokerages that will allow you to buy and sell. Also, depending on the coin, you can become active in the community and be a miner who helps validate transactions on the blockchain network. I won't cover mining in this book, but if you are interested in that, there are a lot of resources online that walk you through how to set up and start mining. You can also invest in non-fungible tokens (NFTs), which are also typically tied to a blockchain and can be purchased with cryptocurrency. As with cryptocurrency, people typically buy NFTs with the goal that they will appreciate in value and then be sold for a profit. NFTs are also covered in great detail online, so I encourage you to do additional research if this is an area you are interested in. Make sure you check with your accountant before investing in cryptocurrency/NFT to understand the impact on your taxes.

TAX STRATEGIES

As you grow your wealth, taxes will become a key consideration to ensure you are maximizing your gains and optimizing all available tax benefits. Before we dive into the topic, I want to cover some fundamentals to explain how different strategies will impact your taxes. For the sake of this chapter and book, I'll be focusing on federal taxes, but some of these strategies could also be relevant to state taxes if you are liable for income tax in your state.

TAX BRACKETS

Governments typically charge people different rates of tax based on how much they earn, with each range of taxable income assigned a different 'tax bracket'. Let's look at the 2022 tax brackets in the United States for single/unmarried individuals:

Taxable income	Tax rate
$0 – $10,275	10%
$10,276 – $41,775	$1,027.50 + 12% of the amount over $10,275
$41,776 – $89,075	$4,807.50 + 22% of the amount over $41,775
$89,076 – $170,050	$15,213.50 + 24% of the amount over $89,075
$170,051 – $215,950	$34,647.50 + 32% of the amount over $170,050
$215,951 – $539,900	$49,335.50 + 35% of the amount over $215,950

$539,901 or more	$162,718 + 37% of the amount over $539,900

Let's say you make $35,000 per year in gross income (meaning before any taxes or deductions are taken out of your paycheck) and you file as a single/unmarried individual. Based on the tax brackets laid out above, you'll pay 10% for the first $10,275 you earn, which comes to $1,027.50. Then for the remaining $24,725 of your income, you will pay 12% tax, which comes to $2,967. Add this to the initial $1,027.50, and your total federal tax bill can be estimated at $3,994.50. Bear in mind however that employers usually take a certain amount of tax out of your paycheck every month and pay it directly to the government, so you will probably have paid some or all of your annual tax bill by the end of the year. When you come to file your taxes, simply enter how much you have paid in taxes over the past year (this is shown on your W2 slip from your employer) and that will be tallied against how much you should have paid the federal government. If you have paid more than needed, you will probably get a refund. If you didn't pay enough, you'll have to pay the difference to the government.

As your income rises and you move into higher tax brackets, you have to pay a higher percentage of your earnings to the government. To help lower your tax bill, there are deductions, credits, and other tax strategies that reduce your adjusted gross income (AGI), which is what the federal government uses to determine how much of your income is taxable. Note that you will become ineligible for some tax deductions and credits if your AGI exceeds a certain amount, so you will not be able to claim them. Once again, please consult an accountant to ensure that you are planning your taxes properly and getting all the benefits available to you, especially at the state level (which I don't cover in this book).

Optimizing your paycheck for taxes

One of the first things you should consider is optimizing your paycheck to reduce your taxable income. This will also align with the investment ideas I introduced earlier and help support your goals. Here are a few ways you can do this:

1. Contribute pre-tax dollars to a retirement account, such as a 401k. This will reduce the gross taxable income in your paycheck while also growing your retirement savings.

2. Contribute to a health savings account (HSA). As with a 401k, an HSA allows you to contribute pre-tax dollars, which reduces your gross taxable income.

Standard deduction/ tax deductions

A tax deduction is an expense that can be subtracted from your taxable income to reduce your tax bill. When filing taxes, you have the choice of accepting the standard deduction provided by IRS or itemizing deductions. For 2022, the standard deduction for a single individual is set at $12,950, which means you can reduce your taxable income by that much. If you have deductions that exceed that amount, you should itemize them to reduce your taxable income even more. Examples of expenses that you can itemize as deductions if the total exceeds the standard deduction include student loan interest, mortgage interest, and charitable contributions. Note that everyone's tax situation is different so, before making any plans, check with your accountant which expenses you can itemize and what impact this will have on your taxes.

Tax credits

Tax credits are another way to reduce the amount of taxes you pay or increase any refund you are due. While deductions reduce your taxable income, tax credits act like a credit against the taxes that you've paid or have to pay. Note that it is good to have a chat with your accountant at the beginning of the tax year so you can evaluate which tax credits might be available to you and how to ensure you qualify for them. For example, sometimes you have to purchase products to get the tax credit. This is the case with electric vehicle tax credits. For some tax credits, your family situation determines whether you qualify. For instance, you need to have children to qualify for child tax credits.

Tax loss harvesting

As highlighted in the chapter on trading, when you sell investments for a gain, the profit qualifies as capital gains and is taxed accordingly. One way to reduce the tax you pay on such profits is to sell investments that aren't doing well, take a loss for them, and offset them against your other capital gains. For example, let's say you buy 100 shares of ACME for $10 and you sell them for $12 per share, making $200 in capital gains. Let's say you also have 100 shares of WIDGET that you also paid $10 for but which are now worth $8. If you sell the WIDGET shares for $8 each, you'll lose $200 on that sale, but will effectively wipe out the capital gains from your ACME sale. This type of strategy is called tax loss harvesting and is typically employed towards the end of the calendar year when you can evaluate how many gains you have to offset and the state of your portfolio. As you grow your portfolio, be very mindful of gains and how they will impact your tax situation. As a reminder, short-term capital gains are taxed at a higher rate than long-term capital gains, so also be mindful of how long you've held investments before you decide to sell them.

Real estate and taxes

There are various ways to get tax benefits from real estate. As always, confirm with an accountant or tax lawyer to verify if these benefits would pertain to you and your tax situation. I'll break down the benefits by primary/secondary home and then by rental, as they each have different benefits – while the tax benefit may apply to one type of investment, it may not apply to the other.

Real estate primary/ secondary property tax benefits

The first tax benefit available from primary and secondary properties is to write off the interest you pay the bank if you have a mortgage. Depending on how much interest you pay, this is one of the main things that might increase your qualifying tax deductions to the point where you can itemize them. When you go to sell your primary/secondary property, you can also itemize and deduct expenses for any improvements you've made. This will reduce your overall taxable income from the sale of the property and is why I recommend keeping track of all expenses related to your property so you can review them with your accountant when you file taxes after selling it.

There are also tax credits available for making improvements to your home that optimize energy efficiency, such as installing energy-efficient systems like a furnace, increasing the insulation in your walls, or installing better-insulated windows. One improvement that can pay for itself quickly, depending on where your property is located and how much sun it gets, is installing renewable energy systems like solar power panels. This helps reduce your energy bills and might increase the value of your property when it comes time to sell. You need to evaluate the upfront cost of these expenses and make sure the gains that you will realize for energy savings will occur during your ownership of the property. If you don't realize the gains, you can evaluate if it makes sense for you and if it would help with selling. In all these cases, incentives may also be available through your state or utility provider, so make sure you research those and factor them into your decision.

Rental property tax strategies

The tax strategies for rental properties more closely mirror those of business tax than personal tax. Your rental property will probably generate income in the form of monthly rent, and you'll have expenses that offset some of that income. Also, rental properties are an asset that can be depreciated, which also reduces your overall taxable income. If you eventually want to sell your rental property, you can also do a 1031 exchange. This is a way to roll the proceeds of the sale into a new rental property of equal or greater value, thereby deferring the taxes you'd have to recognize with the sale of the rental property. There are a lot of nuances to a 1031 exchange and they involve a lot time-sensitive steps, so make sure you work with a real estate professional, accountant and lender that is familiar with them.

Borrowing against assets

As you build up your portfolio of investments, whether they are securities, rentals or something else, there may come a time when you'd like liquidity, but don't want to sell the investments. This is when borrowing against your assets can come in handy – albeit with a heavy dose of caution. If you have securities in a brokerage account, you can sometimes set up a margin account that allows you to borrow money against your investments. When you do this, you are borrowing money from the brokerage and using the assets as collateral. This means that if you are unable to pay the brokerage back, they will sell your assets to recoup the margin loan. First, verify that your brokerage supports this. Also be mindful of the interest rates they charge, as high rates can defeat the purpose of borrowing against assets. But if the interest rate is good and your assets are fairly stable, it could be an option to explore. The neat thing about margin loans is they don't qualify as income. You don't pay taxes on the money to get the loan, you continue benefiting from a well-performing investment, and you don't take the tax burden associated with selling the asset at a gain. If your assets drop in value significantly, a margin call can occur, which will require you to deposit more money into the brokerage account to secure the loan. Volatility in the value of your assets can also put you in a pickle here, so it is good to review this with a financial advisor to see if a margin loan makes sense.

With rental properties, or even your primary/ secondary home, you can also do a cash-out refinance, which allows you to refinance your mortgage and take out some of the equity you have in the property. Whether this is possible or makes sense depends on how much equity you have. The lender will most likely require you to retain a minimum of 20% equity in the property. If there has been a boom in the housing market where you own property, the valuation of your property may rise enough for you to have more equity. Note that a cash-out refinance will probably increase your monthly mortgage payment, so make sure you run the numbers with a financial advisor and a lender to ensure you can handle this. As with a margin loan, taxes are not applied to the money you take out with a cash-out refinance because it is essentially a loan.

Another way to get money from your property is through a home equity line of credit (HELOC). As with a cash-out refinance, this uses equity you have in your property to issue you a loan. Typically, HELOCs are used to make improvements to the property you are borrowing against, in which case interest you pay may be deductible as a tax benefit. If you plan to use a HELOC for something else, verify with your lender that this is allowed, and check with your accountant that you can deduct the interest.

These strategies are typically used by the wealthy to

access extra money while ensuring they don't lose stakes in companies or investments they own or take a big tax hit on capital gains.

START A BUSINESS/
SIDE HUSTLE

Starting a business or side hustle allows you to invest in a passion or career that might increase your earning potential. There are many books/tutorials out there that highlight business ideas you could do on the side or talk you through how to start a business from scratch. If you start a side hustle, it may still make sense to establish a legal business entity. The simplest way is to set up as a sole proprietorship, which allows you to operate as a business but doesn't offer as much liability protection as structures like limited liability corporations. Make sure you evaluate the longevity of the venture you are pursuing and whether you want to build it for the long term or see it as a short-term project. If you have long-term ambitions and there is the chance that you will expand by hiring people, I encourage you to investigate setting up a legal business entity so you have a proper structure for running your business.

Here are some examples of side hustles that you can generate income from:

- Writing a blog and monetizing through advertising or sponsorship
- Growing followers on a social network and

monetizing through sponsorship

- Writing a book
- Creating art like pictures, sculptures, or music
- Selling things you make through online marketplaces like Etsy
- Reselling items through online marketplaces like Amazon or eBay.

I find it helpful to list the pros and cons of starting a side hustle/business so you can weigh up the risks involved and reduce the chances of being blindsided by a con once you get started.

Here are some potential pros:

- You have the chance to generate income that will help you reach your goals more quickly
- You can pursue things you are passionate about, which will give you energy and add excitement to your life
- If you don't like your full-time job, you may be able to generate enough income to do the side hustle/business full time
- Pride as you grow your side hustle/business
- You get to overcome challenges, which allows you to be creative.

Here are some potential cons:

- There may be upfront costs that make you less financially secure
- Side hustles/businesses require time and effort to generate income, so make sure you have enough time to spare.
- There are additional tax considerations, so make sure you talk to an accountant to identify the impact.
- The amount of time and money you have to invest may not return as much money as your full-time job
- You may be doing this by yourself, which can be lonely, so make sure you find support from friends and family.

There may be additional cons that you need to consider depending on what your side hustle/business is. List these cons and make a plan for how you will address them.

INVEST IN YOURSELF

Investing in yourself is really rewarding and can also lead to financial gains. Any career/profession offers the chance of growth/learning that will make you better at what you do or allow you to take on more responsibility, which can lead to raises and bonuses. While such financial gains are beneficial, it is also important to identify areas of interest that will help you grow in your personal life and find balance. Remember your goals and make sure that investments you make in yourself align with them.

Financial benefits of investing in yourself

As mentioned, as you improve yourself, you become more marketable and that can lead to promotions, raises and bonuses. This increases your earning potential and can help you take advantage of many of the financial planning strategies covered in this book. As you investigate areas of learning/growth, check with the company you work for and see if they offer any education/continuing education reimbursement. Some of my jobs have offered to reimburse employees up to a specific amount for continuing education, including getting a Bachelor or Master degree, which will stay with you and make you a lot more promotable. Master degrees also open up more work opportunities, such as the ability to teach college classes. If your company doesn't offer reimbursement, you may still be able to get tax benefits such as education tax credits or deductions that will help offset your education expenses. Check with your accountant if you are eligible for these. And even if you don't qualify, it is still worthwhile to pursue things you are passionate about and to constantly be learning and growing. The IRS includes information about education tax credits and deductions that will help offset education expenses.

LIFE INSURANCE

Life insurance is an insurance policy that pays out an agreed amount of money upon your death to cover your debts or support any dependents. Life insurance is often included with your job and you may be able to increase the amount of money that is paid out upon your death by paying a bit more each month out of your paycheck. Life insurance has historically been structured where you pay a premium and receive coverage for a specified amount of time. There are two main types: term life insurance, which covers you for a specific number of years; and permanent (ex: whole life, universal life, etc) which doesn't expire as long as you continue paying the premiums. Life insurance is mainly focused on protecting assets after death, so it is a longer-term strategy. With some life insurance policies, you can also build equity in the policy, which you can borrow against or withdraw in the future without closing the policy. If you have dependents, review with an insurance broker or your human resources department which life insurance policies are available to you and fit your family circumstances best.

LEGAL DOCUMENTS

It is never too early to make sure you have proper legal protection for your assets. There are 3 main legal documents that you should have: Will, Health Care Directive, and Power of Attorney. At a high level, these documents will ensure your interests are protected and that if something happens where you are unable to make decisions, your wishes will be honored. I'll provide links to more details about these on the resources site, but I encourage you to establish these documents if you don't have them already.

CONCLUSION AND RECAP

Financial literacy is so critical in this day and age, and our first interaction with it is too often in reaction to a life event. I hope this book has provided a high-level overview of financial planning so you can get started on your plan without getting overwhelmed. As I highlight frequently in the book, it is good to find a trusted financial advisor, legal advisor, accountant, and bank to aid you in your financial journey. These people/organizations will play a critical role in your success, so make sure you select yours carefully, and don't be afraid to switch to another if they aren't helping as you expected. Also be sure to review the resources I pulled together on https://www.coreyganser.com/finance-book so that you can go deeper in specific topics of interest. If you found this book helpful, please share/recommend it with other people in your life. Thank you for reading and I wish you nothing but success on your journey.

TERMINOLOGY

- **AGI** – Adjusted gross income is the final amount of income that you are taxed on. This is calculated after all deductions and other tax considerations are applied. A good tax strategy is to identify ways to lower your AGI, some of which we'll cover in this book.

- **Capital gains** – When you liquidate an investment, there will either be a loss or gain. These typically are categorized as capital gains and may have a different tax rate applied to them, depending on your tax situation and the nature of the investment that you liquidated.

- **Compound interest** – The interest on savings calculated on both the initial principal and the accumulated interest from previous periods. For example, imagine you have an account with $1,000 in it. Let's say the interest rate that is applied monthly is 0.25%. You will receive $2.50 of interest in the first month, which will increase your balance to $1,002.50. The next time interest is calculated, it will be on the $1,002.50, so you will be paid interest on the $2.50 that you received in the previous month. This allows your account to grow even more as you receive interest on your interest.

- **Equity** – When looking at an investment, the core

value of it that you own is your equity. Equity can change over time depending on the investment.

- **ESG** – This refers to a category of investments where the underlying assets comply or align with specific environment, social or governance (ESG) goals. An investor can also have an ESG strategy where they trade specific companies or investments that align with their specific ESG focus.
- **Fixed rate** – An interest rate that doesn't change for the duration of a loan.
- **Fund** – A collection of multiple securities grouped together under a common theme/goal.
- **Index** – Also known as a market index, this is a portfolio of investments in securities that are chosen to represent a portion of the financial market.
- **Investment portfolio** – Name given to a grouping of your investments. Typically, it is representative of all of your investments.
- **Liquidity** – The liquidity of an investment describes how easy it would be to convert it back into cash that you can use to buy something else.
- **Net investment income** – The amount of profit you get from your investments after all fees and losses are subtracted.
- **Principal** – The initial size of a loan or a bond (the amount that must be repaid).
- **RMD** – Required minimum distribution is the

minimum amount that needs to be withdrawn for specific retirement accounts. If the retirement account has an RMD, you are required to start withdrawing that minimum amount each specified period until the funds are completely disbursed.

- **ROI** – Return on investment reflects how much you will get back for your money, time or other resources.

- **Securities** – A financial entity that represents a monetary value. In this book, we cover common securities like stocks, bonds, and options. Investopedia is a good resource for learning more about securities.